THE ANTI-ANXIETY NOTEBOOK
Cognitive Behavioral Therapy to Reframe and Reset

Designed by therapists to help you discover effective tools for
managing anxiety.

. . . .
(THIS BOOK BELONGS TO)

. . . .
(IF FOUND, PLEASE RETURN TO)

LEARN MORE
www.therapynotebooks.com

THERAPY NOTEBOOKS
Published by Subject Matters

ISBN: 9781735084688
Printed in the United States of America

LEAD THERAPIST
Hod Tamir, PhD

EDITED BY
Rachel E. Brenner, PhD
Diana Hu, PsyD
Emory Strickland, PsyD
Haley Nahman

DESIGNED BY
Monumento.Co

BRANDING BY
High Tide

IF YOU ARE IN URGENT
NEED OF ASSISTANCE:
Dial 9-1-1

FOR MENTAL HEALTH
CRISIS SUPPORT:
Dial 9-8-8

SAMHSA National Helpline
1-800-622-HELP (4357)

Crisis Text Line
Text HOME to 741741

Some Guiding Principles

This journal is designed so you can start right away
if you wish. You can find additional guidance in the
Introduction and Appendices.

1   How will this journal help with anxiety?

        In this journal, you will practice becoming aware of the relation-
        ship between your thoughts and your feelings, empowering you
        to challenge and adjust them over time.

2   When should I use this journal?

        Whenever you feel anxious or stressed, but there's no pressure.
        You can use this however often you feel comfortable, whether
        that's daily or on an as-needed basis.

3   How does Cognitive Behavioral Therapy fit in?

        CBT is considered the "gold standard" of therapy for managing
        anxiety.[1] The format of the journal entries is based on a common
        CBT exercise designed to help you identify, challenge, and adjust
        your thinking patterns.

Letter From a Therapist

If you've picked up this journal, odds are that you're feeling anxious or stressed, and you're not alone. Forty million people in the United States struggle with anxiety disorders, and many more deal with some form of anxiety in their lifetime. With the onslaught of information coming at us from all directions and so many things to occupy us with worry, it's hard not to be anxious today.

As a developmental psychologist, researcher, and professor, I have spent the past decade studying mental health, anxiety, and well-being through different lenses. Dealing with anxiety has not only been a professional pursuit but a personal endeavor. Having grappled for many years with social anxiety and avoidance myself, I know how deeply anxiety can impact daily life.

Fortunately, clinicians and researchers have developed and rigorously tested a range of effective tools for managing our anxiety. But in comparing my research collaborations to my conversations with students and clients, I've always been struck by the accessibility gap. Even though we know of tools backed by hundreds of peer-reviewed studies, many of those tools have not moved from the world of research to everyday use. Traditional therapy textbooks and workbooks are often too clunky and clinical, while the self-help genre has very few requirements for evidence-based rigor, and considerable stigma continues to hinder access.

Together with a few colleagues, I sought to create something to bridge this gap—a resource that would make effective tools more accessible for my clients, my students, and, ideally, anyone dealing with anxiety. Our goal was to develop a resource not only supported by clinicians and science, but genuinely enjoyable to use. That's how this journal came to be.

Our intention is to help you learn and practice evidence-based tools for managing anxiety, with an emphasis on Cognitive Behavioral Therapy. Since managing anxiety is not a one-size-fits-all regimen, we want to empower you to find the tools that work for you, understand how your mind works, recognize unhelpful patterns, and challenge yourself to think differently.

We hope you take a moment to recognize that simply starting this journal is a big step forward. It can be unsettling to move beyond your comfort zone and I applaud your willingness to try something new and invite change into your life. This is not a magic book—it will not miraculously make your problems disappear—but it will help you reflect, direct your writing, and provide effective tools and insights along the way. I hope it will remind you that you are capable of positive change. Every page you complete in this journal is an act of strength and courage. I'll be rooting for you.

Sincerely,

Hod Tamir, PhD
Lead Therapist

Scan the QR code to meet our clinicians

How This Book Helps You

1   Practice the *gold standard* for managing anxiety:
        Cognitive Behavioral Therapy.

        The Anti-Anxiety Notebook relies on the most well-researched
        and effective form of psychotherapy used by millions. You'll
        learn how thoughts shape your emotions, and how to recognize
        and change unhelpful thought patterns.

2   The right amount of structure and freedom to support your
        journaling.

        Blank pages are daunting, and filling all that negative space
        can leave you at a loss for words. We've worked with experts to
        provide the right balance of structure and freedom to empower
        you to process your emotions and experiences effectively.

3   Find calm by recognizing and challenging unhelpful thought
        patterns.

        Anxiety makes it difficult to pay attention to the present
        moment. Instead of focusing on what is within your control,
        you might fixate and obsess while your stress levels climb. This
        notebook helps you address the unhelpful thoughts that escalate
        your emotions.

4   Discover the science behind the most effective evidence-based
        tools.

        We've distilled hundreds of peer-reviewed articles into an
        easy-to-read experience. Not only will you learn how to put the
        most well-researched tools for combatting anxiety into practice,
        you'll also come to understand why and how they work.

5   Made by therapists who have helped countless clients put these
        tools into practice.

        The clinicians behind The Anti-Anxiety Notebook have years of
        experience using these tools and techniques to help clients combat
        their anxiety and transform their lives—and now you can, too.

Contents

I INTRODUCTION:
Anxiety and Evidence-Based Tools

Imagine trying to focus with several people talking to you at once—this is what anxiety can feel like, only the voices are your own. It's very human to want to escape this feeling: to plug your ears, drown it out, pray for it to just stop. But anxiety isn't just noise; if you listen closely, you'll find it follows a certain logic. In that way, it can be helpful to tune into it, rather than tune it out. By learning to apply the core tenets of Cognitive Behavioral Therapy and other evidence-based tools that professionals use with great success, you will likely find that you are far more capable of managing your own anxiety than you thought possible.

DEFINING ANXIETY

Before we can think about treating anxiety, it helps to understand what it is and why we feel it. First, the "what." Anxiety is characterized by excessive worry that is difficult to control, ruminating on the past, or avoiding things we fear might trigger us further. It can also induce physical symptoms such as increased heart rate, restlessness, difficulty concentrating, changes in sleep and appetite, and general bodily tension. This heightened state can interrupt our lives in ways big and small, and can impact our ability to manage our own emotions.

Second, the "why." Anxiety is an adaptive instinct that signals that we may be in danger. It's our mind's way of telling our body to prepare for fight or flight. Of course, when danger is actually imminent, this is helpful, but when this neural mechanism gets overused and overapplied to non-threatening scenarios, we're left with a bodily response that doesn't quite fit the situation. Research has shown that when we feel anxious, the part of our brain that regulates our moods and helps us make good decisions, known as the prefrontal cortex, is less active, while the part of our brain that produces a fear response, the amygdala, is overactive. This is why anxiety can feel overwhelming—our more regulatory instincts take a backseat to our fears and worries. Luckily, there are many research-backed strategies for responding to anxiety that can help us rewire some of these unhelpful neural relationships.

THE ROLE OF COGNITIVE BEHAVIORAL THERAPY

Cognitive Behavioral Therapy, known as CBT, was developed by psychiatrist Aaron Beck in the 1960s. He noticed that his clients often engaged in destructive thought patterns that negatively affected their feelings and behaviors. He reasoned that if they could change the stories they told themselves, their resulting feelings and behaviors might change, too. This became the founding principle of CBT: we are governed more by our perceptions of reality than by reality itself, and so by changing our perceptions, we can feel entirely differently than we did before. CBT is now considered the most effective therapy for anxiety, along with several other mental health conditions.[2]

Imagine, for example, that you are nervous about starting a new job. Perhaps you start worrying that your coworkers won't like you, or that you won't be competent enough to do what's expected of you. This then sets off a fear response in your body that suppresses your ability to consider what might go well. This is how anxiety can begin to grip your mind, warping your reality (that you are starting a new job) into a different one (that you will fail at the job).

Your instinct in this moment might be to avoid these thoughts or ignore important work decisions or not talk to coworkers. Your anxiety is changing your behavior and creating the reality that you feared. CBT would encourage you to respond in a different way: It would ask that you identify the specific thought that triggered your anxiety, and consider where it's coming from and whether it's helpful for you. Are you catastrophizing? Are you magnifying the negative and minimizing the positive? You would then evaluate the facts at hand to consider how you could see the situation differently: more positively, more logically, with fewer assumptions. By challenging your anxious thoughts you can break the cycle and allow yourself to build a counter-narrative—one that can inspire not just a shift in mindset, but impactful changes in your behavior, too.

Throughout this notebook, you'll be going through this very process in writing. Even just the simple act of journaling has been proven in clinical studies to reduce anxiety and depression.[3] By journaling using the CBT framework, you will develop the skills to identify, challenge, and change your unhelpful thought patterns. You may be surprised at what you find: the fears that are warping how you think, the negative beliefs you've been harboring about yourself, and the subtle ways these things inform your worldview.

OTHER EVIDENCE-BASED TOOLS

There's a wide range of evidence that demonstrates the efficacy of CBT for managing anxiety. Throughout this book, you'll learn about a variety of other research-backed tools that are similarly effective. In between each journal entry, you will find five check-ins, each of which explores a different tool and its unique relationship with mental health. Specifically, you will learn about mindset, breath, sleep, relationships, and distraction—each with accompanying clinical studies. You'll learn how just one minute of mindful breathing can decrease your brain's fear response, why a full night's rest matters for your ability to make sound decisions, and how to make distraction work for your brain rather than against it. These topics were chosen for their significant yet underutilized findings, and they are a window into the many ways you can learn to better manage your mental health in everyday life.

By picking up this notebook, you've already done something important: you've recognized that something needs to change. That is a powerful realization that can't be discounted. Throughout this process, you will learn to write new stories about who you are, how you react, and what is possible. There is no version of reality that does not include unforeseen challenges, but with the right tools, you'll discover just how resilient you are, and that is no small feat.

Let's get started.

TIPS

- Journal entries are designed to be intuitive and easy to use. However, we recommend you at least skim through the CBT Basics, Cognitive Distortions, and Feelings Wheel sections in the Appendices and consult them whenever you need to.

- The check-ins are provided to help you pause and reflect. They introduce evidence-based tools for anxiety and provide tips and questions to help you integrate those tools into your life.

- The purpose of this journal is to help you process your emotions and experiences in a constructive way. It is designed to give you full autonomy; you can start however you want, go in order or not, and pick up whenever or wherever. We generally recommend using the journal entries whenever you feel anxious or stressed in order to best identify, track, and improve patterns in your thinking.

1   Setting a specific intention can help guide you consciously and
      subconsciously. What purpose do you hope this notebook will
      serve? What do you hope to get out of using it? Be as concrete or
      abstract as feels right.

2   The below questions are from the GAD-7 scale, one of the
     tools used by therapists to measure anxiety. We will revisit this
     scale at the end of the journal so that you can see how you've
     progressed over time.

OVER THE LAST 2 WEEKS, HOW OFTEN HAVE YOU BEEN BOTHERED BY THE FOLLOWING?	NONE/ NOT SURE	SEVERAL DAYS	OVER HALF THE DAYS	NEARLY DAILY
Feeling nervous, anxious, or on edge	0	1	2	3
Not being able to stop or control worrying	0	1	2	3
Worrying too much about different things	0	1	2	3
Trouble relaxing	0	1	2	3
Being so restless it's hard to sit still	0	1	2	3
Becoming easily annoyed or irritable	0	1	2	3
Feeling as if something awful might happen	0	1	2	3
Add the score for each column		+	+	+
Total Score				

3   We often know more about what is going on in our minds than
     we realize. What are the major events, relationships, or thoughts
     that you currently identify as persistent sources of anxiety or
     worry? Are there certain patterns or sources of anxiety that
     you've already observed?

Your Journal Entries

1   What happened?   (Describe the situation)

Try to focus on the facts (who, what, when, where). Be brief and specific. The smaller the moment in time you can pinpoint, the better you'll understand the emotions and reactions that followed. For instance, "the boss called on me for an idea" is more effective than "Monday morning meeting."

2   What is going through your mind?   (Describe the situation)

Put yourself back in that moment and note the thoughts that were in your head. Identifying your thoughts is a foundational aspect of CBT. Instead of dismissing your thoughts (e.g. "it really wasn't that big of a deal"), allow them to flow honestly.

3   What emotions are you feeling?   (Note the intensity)

Name the various emotions you felt in that moment. Rate their intensity on a scale from 1 (barely feeling the emotion) to 10 (most intensely you've ever felt this way). Do your best to avoid listing "anxious." Use the Feelings Wheel in Appendix C for help.

4   What thought patterns do you recognize?   (Circle any or write your own)

All or nothing   Fortune telling   Minimizing the positive
Blaming others   Labeling   Overgeneralization
Catastrophizing   Magnifying the negative   Self-blaming
Emotional reasoning   Mind reading   Should statements

Naming our thought patterns makes them less huge, intimidating, and threatening. Identifying these

patterns help us see how our self-talk may be skewed and begin reducing some of the emotional inten-

sity. Consult the Cognitive Distortions section in Appendix B to see definitions of common patterns.

5   How can you think about the situation differently?   (Challenge your thoughts)

Taking a step back from automatically believing our thoughts is the hard work of CBT.

Try to take a more objective, helpful, and self-compassionate look at your thoughts

and patterns. What might a friend, mentor, or coach say? How can you grow from this?

Consult Appendices A and B for more examples of how to reframe your thoughts.

This is your space. We encourage you to use it however you wish.

A few suggestions:

- Draw, sketch, scribble, or free write
- Continue your answers from the previous section
- Reflect on the therapist note on the next page
- List one small concrete action you can take now or later that might make you feel better

NOTE FROM A THERAPIST

These notes will help guide your journaling, provide
additional questions for reflection, or include tips for
incorporating more tools into your life.

1   What happened?   (Describe the situation)

At dinner, Jesse's mom made a joke about my job. Something about being an hourly worker. The whole family was there and everyone laughed.

2   What is going through your mind?   (Describe the situation)

I immediately thought, why did she say that? Does everyone think I have a terrible job? I wondered if the entire family thinks I'm mooching off my partner's or that Jesse deserves better. Honestly I thought maybe I really can't get a better job and Jesse might leave me eventually.

3   What emotions are you feeling?   (Note the intensity)

Embarrassed   1 2 3 4 ⑤ 6 7 8 9 10

Self-Conscious   1 2 3 4 5 6 ⑦ 8 9 10

                                                               1 2 3 4 5 6 7 8 9 10

4   What thought patterns do you recognize?   (Circle any or write your own)

All or nothing   ~~Fortune telling~~   Minimizing the positive
~~Blaming others~~   Labeling   Overgeneralization
Catastrophizing   ~~Magnifying the negative~~   Self-blaming
Emotional reasoning   Mind reading   ~~Should statements~~

5   How can you think about the situation differently?   (Challenge your thoughts)

Jesse's mom's comment hurt, but was likely just a joke without bad intentions. And though I do make less than Jesse, I really enjoy my job. I don't really know what Jesse's family thinks of me, but they consistently welcome me into their home and are friendly.

These moments are usually pretty tough for me. I know I spiral and they seem to

happen a lot. I wonder if I should just talk to Jesse's mom about how I feel.

Next time I'll head to the bathroom, splash a little cold water on my face, and focus

on my breathing for a minute.

NOTE FROM A THERAPIST

One helpful way to look at a situation differently is
to think about it from the perspective of a friend.

1   What happened?   (Describe the situation)

2   What is going through your mind?   (Describe the situation)

3   What emotions are you feeling?   (Note the intensity)

1 2 3 4 5 6 7 8 9 10

1 2 3 4 5 6 7 8 9 10

1 2 3 4 5 6 7 8 9 10

4   What thought patterns do you recognize?   (Circle any or write your own)

All or nothing   Fortune telling   Minimizing the positive
Blaming others   Labeling   Overgeneralization
Catastrophizing   Magnifying the negative   Self-blaming
Emotional reasoning   Mind reading   Should statements

5   How can you think about the situation differently?   (Challenge your thoughts)

NOTE FROM A THERAPIST

Sometimes we take for granted that what's in our head is fact. The more you put your thoughts into writing, the more you can challenge them.

1   What happened?   (Describe the situation)

2   What is going through your mind?   (Describe the situation)

3   What emotions are you feeling?   (Note the intensity)

1 2 3 4 5 6 7 8 9 10

1 2 3 4 5 6 7 8 9 10

1 2 3 4 5 6 7 8 9 10

4   What thought patterns do you recognize?   (Circle any or write your own)

All or nothing   Fortune telling   Minimizing the positive
Blaming others   Labeling   Overgeneralization
Catastrophizing   Magnifying the negative   Self-blaming
Emotional reasoning   Mind reading   Should statements

5   How can you think about the situation differently?   (Challenge your thoughts)

NOTE FROM A THERAPIST

A helpful way to reframe your thoughts: ask, "What would ____ say or advise?" Fill the blank with the name of a friend, mentor, parent, or whomever.

1   What happened?   (Describe the situation)

2   What is going through your mind?   (Describe the situation)

3   What emotions are you feeling?   (Note the intensity)

1 2 3 4 5 6 7 8 9 10

1 2 3 4 5 6 7 8 9 10

1 2 3 4 5 6 7 8 9 10

4   What thought patterns do you recognize?   (Circle any or write your own)

All or nothing   Fortune telling   Minimizing the positive
Blaming others   Labeling   Overgeneralization
Catastrophizing   Magnifying the negative   Self-blaming
Emotional reasoning   Mind reading   Should statements

5   How can you think about the situation differently?   (Challenge your thoughts)

NOTE FROM A THERAPIST

In describing what happened, be as objective as
possible. What would an impartial witness say?
What would be upheld in a court of law?

1   What happened?   (Describe the situation)

2   What is going through your mind?   (Describe the situation)

3   What emotions are you feeling?   (Note the intensity)

1 2 3 4 5 6 7 8 9 10

1 2 3 4 5 6 7 8 9 10

1 2 3 4 5 6 7 8 9 10

4   What thought patterns do you recognize?   (Circle any or write your own)

All or nothing   Fortune telling   Minimizing the positive
Blaming others   Labeling   Overgeneralization
Catastrophizing   Magnifying the negative   Self-blaming
Emotional reasoning   Mind reading   Should statements

5   How can you think about the situation differently?   (Challenge your thoughts)

NOTE FROM A THERAPIST

When you don't have the journal handy, use the CBT shortcut: Catch it, Check it, Change it. Observe your thoughts, challenge them, then reframe them.

1   What happened?   (Describe the situation)

2   What is going through your mind?   (Describe the situation)

3   What emotions are you feeling?   (Note the intensity)

1 2 3 4 5 6 7 8 9 10

1 2 3 4 5 6 7 8 9 10

1 2 3 4 5 6 7 8 9 10

4   What thought patterns do you recognize?   (Circle any or write your own)

All or nothing   Fortune telling   Minimizing the positive
Blaming others   Labeling   Overgeneralization
Catastrophizing   Magnifying the negative   Self-blaming
Emotional reasoning   Mind reading   Should statements

5   How can you think about the situation differently?   (Challenge your thoughts)

NOTE FROM A THERAPIST

One way to gauge if you are catastrophizing
is by asking yourself, "Five years from now,
will this matter?"

II   MINDSET:
Change is Possible

Schleider, J. and Weisz, J. (2018).
Single-Session Growth Mindset Intervention for Adolescent
Anxiety and Depression: 9-Month Outcomes of a Randomized Trial.

Change holds a curious place in the human imagination. We revere it as much as we fear it, pursue it as passionately as we avoid it, and even when we want it, we still might shy away from it. In that sense, all of us understand the risky role change plays in our lives. We recognize that, whether we yearn for it or not, change requires something of us—a kind of internal reckoning we may not feel ready for. Fortunately, it's within our power to develop a relationship to change that not only helps us grow, but improves our mental health. And that starts with believing that we are capable of change.

"Can people change?" may be a popular debate, but from a scientific perspective, it's not really a debate at all. The answer is a resounding yes. In fact, a lot of research has examined the many ways our brains are capable of transformation. Physiologically speaking, this is referred to as neuroplasticity, or the brain's ability to form new neural connections in response to stimuli, trauma, or varying life circumstances. Our brains, in other words, are malleable. They undergo change on a daily basis.

The idea of a "growth mindset" was first introduced in the mid-2000s by Stanford psychologist Carol Dweck, who proposed that people either believe themselves capable of change (a growth mindset), or the opposite (a fixed mindset). Recently, scientists are finding this mindset isn't just important for "growth" but also for our mental health. In 2017, Harvard researchers successfully reduced anxiety and depression in children by teaching them about neuroplasticity.[4] Participants were split into two groups, the first of which underwent 30 minutes of standard supportive therapy, and the second of which received 30 minutes of a "growth mindset intervention," in which they learned how the mind and personality are capable of change. After nine months and just the one initial session, researchers found significant improvements in anxiety and depression for kids who received the growth mindset intervention over the control group, underlining the psychological impact of believing change is possible.

This is a core tenet of Cognitive Behavioral Therapy, which posits that thoughts, feelings, and behaviors affect each other—and most importantly, can be changed. When this notebook asks you to identify your emotions and interpret them differently, it's asking you to imagine that you are capable of more than your feelings might lead you to believe. And by writing your thought patterns down, rather than letting them languish abstractly in your mind, you also gain the opportunity to observe them from a distance and ask yourself: is this language indicative of a growth mindset, or a fixed one?

It's natural to feel stuck sometimes. Nurturing a growth mindset means allowing yourself to feel stuck, accepting you aren't (and won't be) perfect, believing mistakes can be opportunities to grow, and above all, understanding that the learning process itself—no matter how much failure it entails—is far more valuable than the end result. These are ideas anyone can learn to live by. They do not require any innate skill or talent; they do not demand that you get it right the first time. They simply ask you to imagine what could be possible if you were capable of real, impactful change—and then believe that you are.

TIPS

- While challenging your thoughts in this journal, you might discover an underlying "fixed mindset" belief about yourself ("I'm a bad friend")—practice catching that belief and re-writing it with a growth mindset ("I can become a more supportive friend by listening more and not jumping to conclusions").

- Pay attention to your words and thoughts; keep tweaking them toward a growth mindset. Whenever you think you cannot do something, replace "not" with "not yet," or "I can't do that" with "I can't do that yet."

- When you have 15 minutes to spare, read some of the research on neuroplasticity.

1   Developing a growth mindset and believing in your capacity for positive change can start with articulating it to yourself. Write out this brief statement below and sign your name: "I believe in myself, I am capable of growth, and I am committed to positive change." Then list some of the specific ways you'd like to grow over the next 6, 12, or 24 months, and one small thing you can do to make progress in each period.

2   Reflect on a moment in your life when you experienced diffi-
     culty or perceived failure. How did you grow from that experi-
     ence? What did you learn? If you could speak to your former
     self, what would you say?

3.1   Look through your last section of journal entries for
       patterns. Are certain situations, thoughts, or feelings more
       distressing or frequent?

3.2   Which approaches for reframing your thoughts are
       working best?

3.3   What's one thing you can do differently for the next section
       of journal entries?

1   What happened?   (Describe the situation)

2   What is going through your mind?   (Describe the situation)

3   What emotions are you feeling?   (Note the intensity)

1 2 3 4 5 6 7 8 9 10

1 2 3 4 5 6 7 8 9 10

1 2 3 4 5 6 7 8 9 10

4   What thought patterns do you recognize?   (Circle any or write your own)

    All or nothing   Fortune telling   Minimizing the positive
    Blaming others   Labeling   Overgeneralization
    Catastrophizing   Magnifying the negative   Self-blaming
    Emotional reasoning   Mind reading   Should statements

5   How can you think about the situation differently?   (Challenge your thoughts)

NOTE FROM A THERAPIST

After a stressful situation, try to think about how
you could have reacted differently and what you can
learn from the situation.

1   What happened?   (Describe the situation)

2   What is going through your mind?   (Describe the situation)

3   What emotions are you feeling?   (Note the intensity)

1 2 3 4 5 6 7 8 9 10

1 2 3 4 5 6 7 8 9 10

1 2 3 4 5 6 7 8 9 10

4   What thought patterns do you recognize?   (Circle any or write your own)

All or nothing   Fortune telling   Minimizing the positive
Blaming others   Labeling   Overgeneralization
Catastrophizing   Magnifying the negative   Self-blaming
Emotional reasoning   Mind reading   Should statements

5   How can you think about the situation differently?   (Challenge your thoughts)

NOTE FROM A THERAPIST

While reframing your thoughts, practice a gentle,
understanding approach with yourself. You cannot
shame yourself into improved mental health.

1   What happened?   (Describe the situation)

2   What is going through your mind?   (Describe the situation)

3   What emotions are you feeling?   (Note the intensity)

1 2 3 4 5 6 7 8 9 10

1 2 3 4 5 6 7 8 9 10

1 2 3 4 5 6 7 8 9 10

4   What thought patterns do you recognize?   (Circle any or write your own)

All or nothing   Fortune telling   Minimizing the positive
Blaming others   Labeling   Overgeneralization
Catastrophizing   Magnifying the negative Self-blaming
Emotional reasoning   Mind reading   Should statements

5   How can you think about the situation differently?   (Challenge your thoughts)

NOTE FROM A THERAPIST

Consider how what just happened might
be a good thing in disguise.

1   What happened?   (Describe the situation)

2   What is going through your mind?   (Describe the situation)

3   What emotions are you feeling?   (Note the intensity)

1 2 3 4 5 6 7 8 9 10

1 2 3 4 5 6 7 8 9 10

1 2 3 4 5 6 7 8 9 10

4   What thought patterns do you recognize?   (Circle any or write your own)

All or nothing   Fortune telling   Minimizing the positive
Blaming others   Labeling   Overgeneralization
Catastrophizing   Magnifying the negative   Self-blaming
Emotional reasoning   Mind reading   Should statements

5   How can you think about the situation differently?   (Challenge your thoughts)

NOTE FROM A THERAPIST

Focus on the things in your life that you can control
and let go of the rest. What's one small thing you
can control in this situation?

1   What happened?   (Describe the situation)

2   What is going through your mind?   (Describe the situation)

3   What emotions are you feeling?   (Note the intensity)

1 2 3 4 5 6 7 8 9 10

1 2 3 4 5 6 7 8 9 10

1 2 3 4 5 6 7 8 9 10

4   What thought patterns do you recognize?   (Circle any or write your own)

All or nothing   Fortune telling   Minimizing the positive
Blaming others   Labeling   Overgeneralization
Catastrophizing   Magnifying the negative Self-blaming
Emotional reasoning   Mind reading   Should statements

5   How can you think about the situation differently?   (Challenge your thoughts)

NOTE FROM A THERAPIST

Your expectations often affect the outcome. How did that play out here? What are some positive expectations you can set for next time?

III MINDFULNESS:
The Power of Breath

Zaccaro, A., Piarulli, A., Laurino, M., Garbella, E.,
Menicucci, D., Neri, B., Gemignani, A. (2018).
How Breath-Control Can Change Your Life:
A Systematic Review on Psycho-Physiological Correlates of
Slow Breathing. Frontiers in Human Neuroscience, 12, 353.

Our minds move fast. A smell triggers a memory; a word reminds us of an errand; a sound makes us jump, our bodies preparing, in a split second, to fight or flee. In this way, our natural mental state is like a revolving door, welcoming in new ideas with little security. The result is a whirring mind capable of making up stories and far-flung connections. This mental agility is an important component of our imaginations, but it comes at a price: if we're not careful, we can lose touch with the world around us, and this is a path to anxiety.

Mindfulness allows us to bring ourselves back to earth. The concept can seem intimidating, but mindfulness is really no more than being present. When we are mindful, we are not dwelling in the past nor fantasizing about the future, we are simply aware of the current moment: the ground beneath our feet, the beat of our heart, the rhythm of our breath. Most of us are at least passively aware that this can calm us down, but may not realize that mindfulness, in fact, changes our brains.

In 2018, researchers reviewed the results of 15 different experiments investigating "active breath control"—a conscious breathing pace of no more than 10 breaths a minute, like you might do during yoga—to triangulate common themes.[5] In nearly every case, breath control increased activity in the parasympathetic nervous system, which triggers rest and relaxation. There were also signs of increased activity in regions of the brain associated with attention and emotional control. Perhaps most importantly, the subjects themselves reported an increase in comfort and relaxation, and a reduction in anxiety and depression. All this from as little as one-to-five minutes of active breath control.

Breath control is just one element of mindfulness, but when the world around us buzzes with distraction, it's one of the easiest ways to remain present. Anxiety can hijack the way we think about the past or approach the future, but when we focus on our breath, we're forced to reign in those wandering thoughts, returning instead to one of our core functions. The benefits of mindfulness are always available to us, no matter where we are: all we have to do is listen to ourselves breathe.

Next time you find yourself overwhelmed by all the emails in your inbox, the bus you just missed, or an approaching deadline at work, try box breathing, a relaxation technique used by healthcare providers to calm the mind: breathe in for four counts, hold for four counts, breathe out for four counts, repeat. Or, if you favor an even more straightforward approach, simply turn your attention to your breaths, counting each one as you take it. These practices might feel insignificant, but they nourish our bodies and brains in ways we may not even register at first. Just like a marathon runner needs water, a racing mind needs rest, and with a little intention, it's ours for the taking.

TIPS

- A single, consciously deep breath can calm you down. Practice the habit of taking a breath when you're stressed. In fact, try to take one before you start each journal entry.

- Try box breathing: slowly breathe in counting to four, hold your breath for four more counts, then breathe out for four counts. Repeat this four times.

- Instead of letting the whirlwind of technology and social media prevent you from being present, try actively scheduling time to attend to them later. Setting aside specific time for it means you can focus on what you're doing now.

1   Another way to engage in mindfulness is to be present
     with our body. Take some deep breaths and pay close
     attention to sensations in your body, scanning from the
     top of your head to the bottom of your feet. Try to release
     tension as you go. List any particular areas that carry
     tension.

2   Before moving on to the next question, practice mindfully
    transitioning. First, list sensations from all five of your
    senses. Then state what you intend to do next.

3.1   Look through your last section of journal entries for
       patterns. Are certain situations, thoughts, or feelings more
       distressing or frequent?

3.2   Which approaches for reframing your thoughts are
       working best?

3.3   What's one thing you can do differently for the next section
       of journal entries?

1   What happened?   (Describe the situation)

2   What is going through your mind?   (Describe the situation)

3   What emotions are you feeling?   (Note the intensity)

1 2 3 4 5 6 7 8 9 10

1 2 3 4 5 6 7 8 9 10

1 2 3 4 5 6 7 8 9 10

4   What thought patterns do you recognize?   (Circle any or write your own)

All or nothing   Fortune telling   Minimizing the positive
Blaming others   Labeling   Overgeneralization
Catastrophizing   Magnifying the negative   Self-blaming
Emotional reasoning   Mind reading   Should statements

5   How can you think about the situation differently?   (Challenge your thoughts)

NOTE FROM A THERAPIST

Your mind will wander, and that's okay.
Pay attention to where it goes; observe it compassionately
and, without judgment, bring your focus back.

1   What happened?   (Describe the situation)

2   What is going through your mind?   (Describe the situation)

3   What emotions are you feeling?   (Note the intensity)

1 2 3 4 5 6 7 8 9 10

1 2 3 4 5 6 7 8 9 10

1 2 3 4 5 6 7 8 9 10

4   What thought patterns do you recognize?   (Circle any or write your own)

All or nothing   Fortune telling   Minimizing the positive
Blaming others   Labeling   Overgeneralization
Catastrophizing   Magnifying the negative   Self-blaming
Emotional reasoning   Mind reading   Should statements

5   How can you think about the situation differently?   (Challenge your thoughts)

NOTE FROM A THERAPIST

Try this mindfulness exercise: note 5 things you
see, 4 things you feel, 3 things you hear, 2 things
you smell, and 1 thing you taste.

1   What happened?   (Describe the situation)

2   What is going through your mind?   (Describe the situation)

3   What emotions are you feeling?   (Note the intensity)

1 2 3 4 5 6 7 8 9 10

1 2 3 4 5 6 7 8 9 10

1 2 3 4 5 6 7 8 9 10

4   What thought patterns do you recognize?   (Circle any or write your own)

All or nothing   Fortune telling   Minimizing the positive
Blaming others   Labeling   Overgeneralization
Catastrophizing   Magnifying the negative   Self-blaming
Emotional reasoning   Mind reading   Should statements

5   How can you think about the situation differently?   (Challenge your thoughts)

NOTE FROM A THERAPIST

Mindfulness is not the state of thinking about
nothing. Rather, it is practicing focus and paying
attention to the present moment.

1   What happened?   (Describe the situation)

2   What is going through your mind?   (Describe the situation)

3   What emotions are you feeling?   (Note the intensity)

1 2 3 4 5 6 7 8 9 10

1 2 3 4 5 6 7 8 9 10

1 2 3 4 5 6 7 8 9 10

4   What thought patterns do you recognize?   (Circle any or write your own)

All or nothing   Fortune telling   Minimizing the positive
Blaming others   Labeling   Overgeneralization
Catastrophizing   Magnifying the negative   Self-blaming
Emotional reasoning   Mind reading   Should statements

5   How can you think about the situation differently?   (Challenge your thoughts)

NOTE FROM A THERAPIST

Try diaphragmatic breathing: breathe deeply into your belly, expanding as you breathe in, then breathe deeply out, pushing the air out of your stomach.

1   What happened?   (Describe the situation)

2   What is going through your mind?   (Describe the situation)

3   What emotions are you feeling?   (Note the intensity)

1 2 3 4 5 6 7 8 9 10

1 2 3 4 5 6 7 8 9 10

1 2 3 4 5 6 7 8 9 10

4   What thought patterns do you recognize?   (Circle any or write your own)

All or nothing   Fortune telling   Minimizing the positive
Blaming others   Labeling   Overgeneralization
Catastrophizing   Magnifying the negative   Self-blaming
Emotional reasoning   Mind reading   Should statements

5   How can you think about the situation differently?   (Challenge your thoughts)

NOTE FROM A THERAPIST

Be mindful of new thoughts you have as you
complete this journal entry. Are they insights,
judgments, or passive observations?

IV   SLEEP:
Overnight Therapy

Ben Simon, E., Rossi, A., Harvey, A.G., Walker, M.P. (2019).
Overanxious and Underslept. Nature Human Behavior,
4(1), 100-110.

Sleep can feel like a lonely pursuit, but like love, joy, and pleasure, our need for it connects us all. When we lay down and close our eyes each night, millions of others are doing the same: breathing deeply, quieting their minds, jerking errant limbs as they drift out of consciousness. Over the next several hours, our bodies go through a series of processes that revive our energy, regulate our hormones, store memories, and give our brains the chance to sort through all the information taken in during the day. Of course, with so much of modern life designed to hold our attention, a good night's rest may seem hard to come by. But a stimulating waking life only underscores the importance of quality sleep—especially for those prone to anxiety.

In an experiment published in the scientific journal Nature Human Behaviour, researchers examined how different kinds of sleep affect our brains.[6] Their study specifically explored the link between deep sleep (also known as "slow wave sleep" that occurs during non-REM cycles) and our ability to manage anxiety. Deep sleep promotes processes that strengthen our immune system, repair tissue, and consolidate non-emotional memories, and according to the results of the study, without enough of it, two things can happen. The first is a decrease in activity in our medial prefrontal cortex, the part of the brain concerned with regulating our emotions; the second is an increase in activity in the amygdala, the part of the brain that incites protective emotions like fear. Put those two together and anxiety can only go in one direction.

In an unfortunate twist of biology, when we struggle to manage our emotions, we may then have trouble sleeping. In this way, sleep loss and anxiety have a symbiotic relationship, each feeding off the other. This is only useful knowledge insofar as it can motivate us to prioritize sleep when we're feeling anxious—and understand the role rest can play in improving our mental state. According to the study, every minute of deep sleep gained can improve our ability to self-regulate. A good night's rest, then, can serve as a coping mechanism.

The exact components of an optimal sleep environment will differ by person, and simply fixating on trying to sleep may not prove helpful. But Cognitive Behavioral Therapy for Insomnia (CBT-I) suggests you identify behaviors that disrupt your sleep and replace them with healthier ones. This could mean sticking to a consistent sleep schedule that works with your life and natural body clock (even on weekends); avoiding caffeine at least five hours before you plan to go to bed; and establishing a bedtime routine that removes stimulation like screens, sound, and light. It's easy to forget that sleep is about more than abating fatigue; in fact it's closer to a free form of therapy.[7] And most comforting of all, it's a natural process: as long as we give our bodies the opportunity to reap the benefits, they'll know exactly what to do.

TIPS

- Preparing for sleep is key to training your mind to rest: create and practice a nighttime ritual that prepares your mind and body for rest every night. Avoid things that stimulate the body such as sugars, caffeine, and bright lights; include things that are calming such as herbal teas, writing, light stretching, meditation, and warm or minimal lighting.

- If you didn't sleep well last night or feel fatigued, short 10-minute naps can be helpful. Find a quiet nook, put your feet up, and power nap.

- If you are going to use your phone or watch TV before bed, utilize low blue-light night modes when possible (available on most devices), and slowly wean yourself towards less stimulating and more relaxing audio like calming sounds or bedtime stories.

1   The right sleep habits improve our ability to fall asleep and
     the quality of the sleep. What are your sleep habits and
     how do they impact your ability to sleep? What are the
     unhelpful habits that get in the way of sleep? List some
     healthy sleep habits you can try.

2   Sometimes lying in bed without any distractions creates an opportunity for anxious thoughts to spiral. We also might panic about not sleeping, which only further prevents us from falling asleep. List some ways you can rest even if you can't sleep (perhaps a guided sleep meditation or a book on your nightstand).

3.1   Look through your last section of journal entries for
       patterns. Are certain situations, thoughts, or feelings more
       distressing or frequent?

3.2   Which approaches for reframing your thoughts are
       working best?

3.3   What's one thing you can do differently for the next section
       of journal entries?

1   What happened?   (Describe the situation)

2   What is going through your mind?   (Describe the situation)

3   What emotions are you feeling?   (Note the intensity)

1 2 3 4 5 6 7 8 9 10

1 2 3 4 5 6 7 8 9 10

1 2 3 4 5 6 7 8 9 10

4   What thought patterns do you recognize?   (Circle any or write your own)

All or nothing   Fortune telling   Minimizing the positive
Blaming others   Labeling   Overgeneralization
Catastrophizing   Magnifying the negative   Self-blaming
Emotional reasoning   Mind reading   Should statements

5   How can you think about the situation differently?   (Challenge your thoughts)

NOTE FROM A THERAPIST

When racing thoughts keep us awake, it can be helpful to write them down. What's keeping you up at night?

1   What happened?   (Describe the situation)

2   What is going through your mind?   (Describe the situation)

3   What emotions are you feeling?   (Note the intensity)

1 2 3 4 5 6 7 8 9 10

1 2 3 4 5 6 7 8 9 10

1 2 3 4 5 6 7 8 9 10

4   What thought patterns do you recognize?   (Circle any or write your own)

All or nothing   Fortune telling   Minimizing the positive
Blaming others   Labeling   Overgeneralization
Catastrophizing   Magnifying the negative   Self-blaming
Emotional reasoning   Mind reading   Should statements

5   How can you think about the situation differently?   (Challenge your thoughts)

NOTE FROM A THERAPIST

Chocolate actually has a good amount of
caffeine in it. Although it's a great dessert,
avoid it too close to bedtime.

1   What happened?   (Describe the situation)

2   What is going through your mind?   (Describe the situation)

3   What emotions are you feeling?   (Note the intensity)

1 2 3 4 5 6 7 8 9 10

1 2 3 4 5 6 7 8 9 10

1 2 3 4 5 6 7 8 9 10

4   What thought patterns do you recognize?   (Circle any or write your own)

All or nothing   Fortune telling   Minimizing the positive
Blaming others   Labeling   Overgeneralization
Catastrophizing   Magnifying the negative   Self-blaming
Emotional reasoning   Mind reading   Should statements

5   How can you think about the situation differently?   (Challenge your thoughts)

NOTE FROM A THERAPIST

If you find yourself up at night worrying, try using
a restful distraction like calming sounds or a
(boring) audiobook until you feel more tired.

1   What happened?   (Describe the situation)

2   What is going through your mind?   (Describe the situation)

3   What emotions are you feeling?   (Note the intensity)

1 2 3 4 5 6 7 8 9 10

1 2 3 4 5 6 7 8 9 10

1 2 3 4 5 6 7 8 9 10

4   What thought patterns do you recognize?   (Circle any or write your own)

All or nothing   Fortune telling   Minimizing the positive
Blaming others   Labeling   Overgeneralization
Catastrophizing   Magnifying the negative   Self-blaming
Emotional reasoning   Mind reading   Should statements

5   How can you think about the situation differently?   (Challenge your thoughts)

NOTE FROM A THERAPIST

Quickly Google CBT-I (CBT for Insomnia) tips for falling asleep faster and better sleep quality. It's more effective than any available sleep drug.

1   What happened?   (Describe the situation)

2   What is going through your mind?   (Describe the situation)

3   What emotions are you feeling?   (Note the intensity)

1 2 3 4 5 6 7 8 9 10

1 2 3 4 5 6 7 8 9 10

1 2 3 4 5 6 7 8 9 10

4   What though̶ ̶̶erns do you recognize?   (Circle any or write your own)

All or ̶ ̶ ̶/   Fortune telling   Minimizing the positive
Bla̶ ̶ ̶ rs   Labeling   Overgeneralization
C̶ ̶ ̶izing   Magnifying the negative   Self-blaming
̶ ̶ ̶l reasoning   Mind reading   Should statements

5   How can you think about the situation differently?   (Challenge your thoughts)

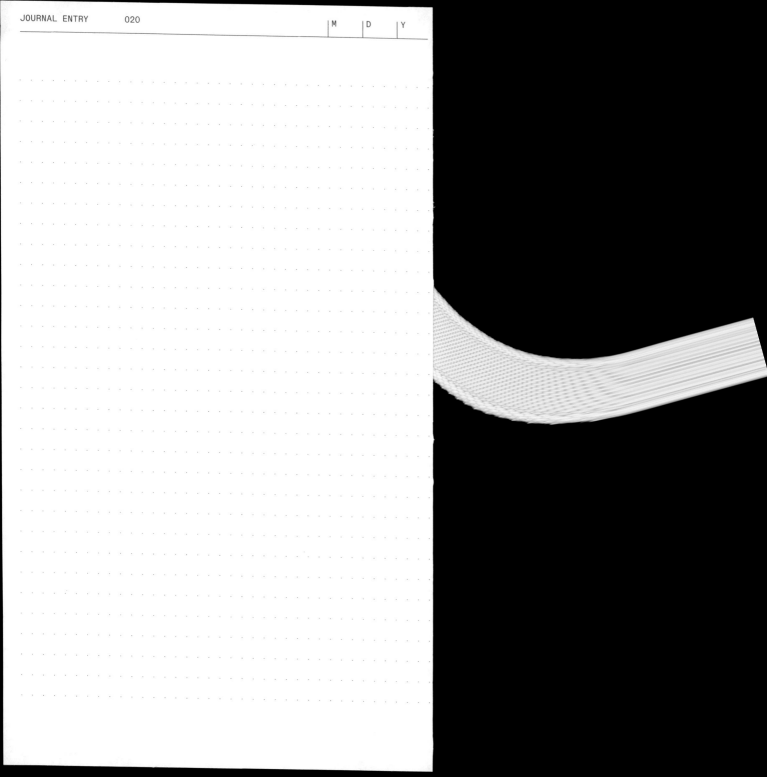

NOTE FROM A THERAPIST

Avoid using your bed for activities other than sleep
or sex. Using it for work or watching TV can make it
harder to relax in bed when you need to.

V   POSITIVE RELATIONSHIPS:
Everyone Needs Support

Siegel, J. Z., Mathys, C., Rutledge, R.B., Crockett, M.J. (2018)
Beliefs About Bad People are Volatile. Nature Human Behaviour,
2(10), 750–756.

If you've ever opted to stay in bed instead of seeing friends, screened calls because you were feeling down, or said you were fine even when you weren't, you know how it feels to withdraw. This is a common response to feeling anxious or depressed. Whether we do it physically or emotionally, many of us prefer to suffer alone. There's nothing wrong with seeking out solitude when we need it, but evidence suggests that, in the long run, there's more to be gained by leaning into our social connections than away from them. Even when it goes against our instincts.

It's hard to quantify the value of friendship, but many scientists have explored its effect on our brains. In a 2011 study, researchers found the part of the brain associated with emotional regulation is larger when we maintain more social connections.[8] Another study found that not only do social connections protect us from stress, they also help us manage it: the very same parts of the brain affected by a good night's rest are affected by a solid social network.[9] There's a reason we feel better after seeing people we love—our brains reward us for it.

But making use of our social networks—whether by asking for help or simply seeking out social nourishment via phone call or text—isn't always so simple. Sometimes our friends and loved ones can drain us, or make us feel worse than we did before. That's when distinguishing between positive and toxic relationships becomes important. "Toxic" is a word that's thrown around a lot, but in this context it simply refers to someone in our lives who is more subtractive than additive. And just as it's hard to underestimate the positive influence quality connections can have on our lives, the same can be said for negative ones.

Most people have encountered at least a few toxic relationships, and there's a psychological explanation for it. One recent study, in which participants were asked to judge two people after they exhibited moral or immoral behavior, found that people are hard-wired to forgive bad behavior, giving people multiple chances to redeem themselves.[10] Scientists believe this gives us room to adjust our expectations when first impressions are wrong, but wielded too freely, it can keep us stuck in relationships that don't serve us. All this is to say: if you have toxic relationships in your life, forgive yourself; it may be a consquence of your compassion. But also keep in mind that by fostering these relationships, you may be directly harming your mental health.

The flipside of our propensity to withhold negative judgment is that we are actually quite good at knowing when someone is a categorically positive presence in our lives. Take a moment and think about the people who make you feel most like yourself—both like the best version of you and also like the one that doesn't need to change to be worthy of love. Make sure to keep these people close, and remember that needing them doesn't make you a burden. It makes you human. Just as you'd likely feel honored if they asked you for help, they'd probably feel the same in return.

TIPS

- Tell your friends and loved ones how they can best support you. For instance, you can clarify that they don't have to fix your anxiety or stress, and that just listening to you is incredibly meaningful.

- Take stock of your current relationships and identify the positive versus potentially toxic ones. Note in particular how you feel when you are with specific people, what types of activities you do together, and how you feel afterward.

- Researchers have found that we get more health benefits from giving support rather than just receiving it.[11] Find ways to actively show compassion to others. When someone reaches out, be there for them as compassionately as you can.

1   What are your biggest barriers to seeking support?
     Common ones include feeling like a burden, concerns
     about being dismissed, and the stigma of asking others
     for help. Do any common thought distortions play a role
     for you in these barriers? How have you developed these
     barriers?

2   What kinds of interactions feel the most connecting
     and gratifying? Think of a current relationship, or even a
     specific interaction with someone where you felt loved,
     appreciated, or valued. What was it about that interaction
     or person that stuck with you? How can you add more of
     that to your life?

3.1   Look through your last section of journal entries for
       patterns. Are certain situations, thoughts, or feelings more
       distressing or frequent?

3.2   Which approaches for reframing your thoughts are
       working best?

3.3   What's one thing you can do differently for the next section
       of journal entries?

1   What happened?   (Describe the situation)

2   What is going through your mind?   (Describe the situation)

3   What emotions are you feeling?   (Note the intensity)

1 2 3 4 5 6 7 8 9 10

1 2 3 4 5 6 7 8 9 10

1 2 3 4 5 6 7 8 9 10

4   What thought patterns do you recognize?   (Circle any or write your own)

All or nothing   Fortune telling   Minimizing the positive
Blaming others   Labeling   Overgeneralization
Catastrophizing   Magnifying the negative   Self-blaming
Emotional reasoning   Mind reading   Should statements

5   How can you think about the situation differently?   (Challenge your thoughts)

NOTE FROM A THERAPIST

Reaching out can include simple things like texting
a funny meme, calling to check in and chat, or
emailing a brief "this made me think of you."

1   What happened?   (Describe the situation)

2   What is going through your mind?   (Describe the situation)

3   What emotions are you feeling?   (Note the intensity)

1 2 3 4 5 6 7 8 9 10

1 2 3 4 5 6 7 8 9 10

1 2 3 4 5 6 7 8 9 10

4   What thought patterns do you recognize?   (Circle any or write your own)

All or nothing   Fortune telling   Minimizing the positive
Blaming others   Labeling   Overgeneralization
Catastrophizing   Magnifying the negative   Self-blaming
Emotional reasoning   Mind reading   Should statements

5   How can you think about the situation differently?   (Challenge your thoughts)

NOTE FROM A THERAPIST

Think about the relationships you find most dependable. Reach out and say thank you. Lean in to those when you need to, maybe even right now.

1   What happened?   (Describe the situation)

2   What is going through your mind?   (Describe the situation)

3   What emotions are you feeling?   (Note the intensity)

1 2 3 4 5 6 7 8 9 10

1 2 3 4 5 6 7 8 9 10

1 2 3 4 5 6 7 8 9 10

4   What thought patterns do you recognize?   (Circle any or write your own)

All or nothing   Fortune telling   Minimizing the positive
Blaming others   Labeling   Overgeneralization
Catastrophizing   Magnifying the negative Self-blaming
Emotional reasoning   Mind reading   Should statements

5   How can you think about the situation differently?   (Challenge your thoughts)

NOTE FROM A THERAPIST

Physical and online communities and support groups are all beneficial. Start building little networks of people you can come back to.

1   What happened?   (Describe the situation)

2   What is going through your mind?   (Describe the situation

3   What emotions are you feeling?   (Note the intensity

1 2 3 4 5 6 7 8 9 10

1 2 3 4 5 6 7 8 9 10

1 2 3 4 5 6 7 8 9 10

4   What thought patterns do you recognize?   (Circle any or write your own)

All or nothing   Fortune telling   Minimizing the positive
Blaming others   Labeling   Overgeneralization
Catastrophizing   Magnifying the negative   Self-blaming
Emotional reasoning   Mind reading   Should statements

5   How can you think about the situation differently?   (Challenge your thoughts)

NOTE FROM A THERAPIST

Build relationships however they work for you. It's just as good to have a few close relationships, many loose-tie relationships, or whatever makes you feel best.

1   What happened?   (Describe the situation)

2   What is going through your mind?   (Describe the situation)

3   What emotions are you feeling?   (Note the intensity)

1 2 3 4 5 6 7 8 9 10

1 2 3 4 5 6 7 8 9 10

1 2 3 4 5 6 7 8 9 10

What thought patterns do you recognize?   (Circle any or write your own)

All or nothing	Fortune telling	Minimizing the positive
Blaming others	Labeling	Overgeneralization
Catastrophizing	Magnifying the negative	Self-blaming
Emotional reasoning	Mind reading	Should statements

How can you think about the situation differently?   (Challenge your thoughts)

NOTE FROM A THERAPIST

What gets in your way of fostering more or closer connections? Is it a self-judgment or fear that you can challenge or reframe?

VI   DISTRACTION:
Distracting Our Minds
Effectively

Bani Mohammad, E., & Ahmad, M. (2019).
Virtual Reality as a Distraction Technique for Pain and Anxiety Among
Patients with Breast Cancer: A Randomized Control Trial. Palliative
and Supportive Care, 17(1), 29–34.

In today's world, we don't look kindly upon distraction. We apologize when our attention wanders, download apps to keep us on task, and tend toward the belief that "paying attention" is always a noble pursuit. But distraction in itself is not a bad thing. In fact, in a clinical environment, distraction is often used to put people's minds at ease or shift their focus.

In a 2018 study, researchers tested the efficacy of distraction as a tool for managing pain and anxiety among cancer patients.[12] Eighty women with breast cancer received morphine for their pain, while half received both morphine and distraction by way of a virtual reality video that brought them deep-sea diving, or to a beach. Perhaps unsurprisingly, the women in the virtual reality group reported a significantly larger decrease in pain and anxiety. This is one of hundreds of studies that have verified distraction as a useful coping mechanism. If you've ever sung a song while getting a shot or jumped around after stubbing your toe, you'll have experienced the effects for yourself.

Distraction is based on a fairly simple principle: anchoring our attention in something neutral or positive is easier than pushing it away from something negative. If we're feeling anxious, it might be easier to manage that anxiety by calling a friend or reading a book than by working through more sophisticated methods (like, for instance, using this notebook). Easier doesn't always mean better, of course, but distraction is a helpful tool when ease is at the forefront of our minds—like when we're feeling low on mental energy, or not quite equipped to deal with something in the present moment. This is when distraction can be employed as a coping mechanism. Sometimes, regaining that sense of ownership over our minds is a crucial step for making other kinds of progress.

To see distraction as a positive force, though, we also have to understand how and why it can be a negative force. Our relationship with avoidance is a good place to start. Most of us use distraction as a means to avoid things we find difficult. This is a natural instinct, but it can lead us away from the things we want, which often requires effort or a tolerance for discomfort. If we make a habit of seeking out distraction whenever those things arise, we may find ourselves stuck, unable to progress or grow. In this way, distraction might make us feel better in the short-term, but it isn't necessarily productive.

Still, temporary relief from something like anxiety can mean a lot when you're struggling. And you should feel empowered to use it when it's not the best time to face something head on. As you've probably learned by working through your emotions in this journal, analyzing our thoughts and feelings requires a lot of mental energy. If we reserve that kind of work for when we're feeling mentally agile, well-rested, bolstered by our social connections, and in the right mindset, we're more likely to experience genuine growth. And when we're not feeling up to it, distraction is a gentler way to take the reins. It's a good reminder that, even when we're feeling anxious, our anxiety doesn't have to control us.

TIPS

- Distraction is effective for managing stress when used appropriately but can quickly become a form of avoidance. To practice using distraction mindfully, try to set a limit on the time or frequency of the distraction.

- Try using calming sensory distractions. For instance, run some cool water over your hands, or mindfully tap your toes or fingers.

- Allow yourself to watch or read something funny and have a laugh. Laughter stimulates organs, releases endorphins, relieves stress, and soothes tension.

1   What are some situations in which you automatically seek
     distraction or shut down in response to rapidly escalating
     emotions? Sometimes distraction is the wise choice.
     Reflect on if that's the case or if there might be better ways
     to react in those situations.

2   Some great distractions are those that also provide a
     growing sense of connection or purpose over time (such
     as painting or team sports). What distractions do you
     usually lean on? Are there other healthy distractions you
     can cultivate in your life?

3.1   Look through your last section of journal entries for
        patterns. Are certain situations, thoughts, or feelings more
        distressing or frequent?

3.2   Which approaches for reframing your thoughts are
       working best?

3.3   What's one thing you can do differently for the next section
       of journal entries?

1   What happened?   (Describe the situation)

2   What is going through your mind?   (Describe the situation)

3   What emotions are you feeling?   (Note the intensity)

1 2 3 4 5 6 7 8 9 10

1 2 3 4 5 6 7 8 9 10

1 2 3 4 5 6 7 8 9 10

4   What thought patterns do you recognize?   (Circle any or write your own)

All or nothing   Fortune telling   Minimizing the positive
Blaming others   Labeling   Overgeneralization
Catastrophizing   Magnifying the negative   Self-blaming
Emotional reasoning   Mind reading   Should statements

5   How can you think about the situation differently?   (Challenge your thoughts)

NOTE FROM A THERAPIST

Have some fun using memory techniques as a distraction: try to remember the address of your home from 10 years ago or the lyrics to a favorite song.

1 What happened? (Describe the situation)

2 What is going through your mind? (Describe the situation)

3 What emotions are you feeling? (Note the intensity)

1 2 3 4 5 6 7 8 9 10

1 2 3 4 5 6 7 8 9 10

1 2 3 4 5 6 7 8 9 10

What thought patterns do you recognize?   (Circle any or write your own)

All or nothing   Fortune telling   Minimizing the positive
Blaming others   Labeling   Overgeneralization
Catastrophizing   Magnifying the negative   Self-blaming
Emotional reasoning   Mind reading   Should statements

How can you think about the situation differently?   (Challenge your thoughts)

NOTE FROM A THERAPIST

Practice using distractions to exercise control over your anxiety. If you're feeling distressed, tell your mind "not now," and move forward.

1   What happened?   (Describe the situation

2   What is going through your mind?   (Describe the situation

3   What emotions are you feeling?   (Note the intensity

1 2 3 4 5 6 7 8 9 1

1 2 3 4 5 6 7 8 9 1

1 2 3 4 5 6 7 8 9 1

4   What thought patterns do you recognize?   (Circle any or write your own)

   All or nothing   Fortune telling   Minimizing the positive
   Blaming others   Labeling   Overgeneralization
   Catastrophizing   Magnifying the negative   Self-blaming
   Emotional reasoning   Mind reading   Should statements

5   How can you think about the situation differently?   (Challenge your thoughts)

NOTE FROM A THERAPIST

When you consider things you might do for distraction, what are the positive and negative thoughts and judgments that might be associated with it?

1   What happened?   (Describe the situation)

2   What is going through your mind?   (Describe the situation)

3   What emotions are you feeling?   (Note the intensity)

1 2 3 4 5 6 7 8 9 10

1 2 3 4 5 6 7 8 9 10

1 2 3 4 5 6 7 8 9 10

4   What thought patterns do you recognize?   (Circle any or write your own)

All or nothing   Fortune telling   Minimizing the positive
Blaming others   Labeling   Overgeneralization
Catastrophizing   Magnifying the negative   Self-blaming
Emotional reasoning   Mind reading   Should statements

5   How can you think about the situation differently?   (Challenge your thoughts)

NOTE FROM A THERAPIST

If you decide to distract yourself, own it. Better to
mindfully say, "I want to enjoy YouTube for the next three
hours" than do it anyway and feel bad afterwards.

1   What happened?   (Describe the situation

2   What is going through your mind?   (Describe the situation

3   What emotions are you feeling?   (Note the intensity

1 2 3 4 5 6 7 8 9 1

1 2 3 4 5 6 7 8 9 1

1 2 3 4 5 6 7 8 9 1

4   What thought patterns do you recognize?   (Circle any or write your own)

All or nothing   Fortune telling   Minimizing the positive
Blaming others   Labeling   Overgeneralization
Catastrophizing   Magnifying the negative   Self-blaming
Emotional reasoning   Mind reading   Should statements

5   How can you think about the situation differently?   (Challenge your thoughts)

NOTE FROM A THERAPIST

Are there certain distractions you use more than
others? When do you most often use them?

Concluding
Check-Out

Congratulations on making it here. Hopefully you're feeling more grounded and better able to catch and reframe your anxiety-provoking thoughts. This final check-out will give you a chance to reflect on how things went and what learnings you can take with you wherever you go.

1   Refer back to your initial check-in and notice what's
            changed. Did you follow through on your belief statement?
            Were your intentions met? Why or why not?

2   How did your answers to these questions change over
           time? What did you notice about changes in your physical
           anxiety symptoms and your awareness of thoughts or
           feelings? Were there changes in how you behaved in
           anxiety-provoking situations?

OVER THE LAST 2 WEEKS, HOW OFTEN HAVE YOU BEEN BOTHERED BY THE FOLLOWING?	NONE/ NOT SURE	SEVERAL DAYS	OVER HALF THE DAYS	NEARLY DAILY
Feeling nervous, anxious, or on edge	0	1	2	3
Not being able to stop or control worrying	0	1	2	3
Worrying too much about different things	0	1	2	3
Trouble relaxing	0	1	2	3
Being so restless it's hard to sit still	0	1	2	3
Becoming easily annoyed or irritable	0	1	2	3
Feeling as if something awful might happen	0	1	2	3
Add the score for each column		+	+	+
Total Score				

3   What are the key thought patterns and distortions you
           observed over the course of journaling? What was partic-
           ularly helpful to remember as you were challenging the
           negative thoughts? What might be able to cue you back to
           that as you move forward?

4   What are three things you've learned, big or small, from this notebook that you want to carry forward with you?

A   CBT Basics

Cognitive Behavioral Therapy (CBT) is based on a simple yet powerful insight: our thoughts impact our feelings. If we learn to better understand and manage our unending trains of thought, we will feel better.

A BRIEF HISTORY

Prior to the development of CBT, psychotherapy was dominated by the belief that painful feelings are caused by early childhood experiences and that the path to relieving those feelings was through analysis that identifies unconscious memories and associations. That branch of therapy is known as psychodynamic therapy and is probably most famous for its founding father, Sigmund Freud. Though this connection between current feelings and early experiences likely exists for many of us, much of modern psychotherapy, driven by the development of CBT, is grounded in identifying and challenging our thinking patterns.

CBT was pioneered in the 1950s and 1960s, and has become the "gold standard" of psychotherapy.[1] Hundreds of studies over the last few decades have shown that CBT can be used to relieve a large variety of problems, especially anxiety and depression, more effectively and quickly than most other therapy modalities.

AUTOMATIC THOUGHTS

CBT posits that most of our thoughts are automatic thoughts that we have formed over time as an immediate response to events. Our minds are constantly interpreting what we see, hear, touch, and feel around us and forming labels, judgments, and predictions based on those observations. Though these automatic thoughts are efficient, they are formed without reflection or deliberate reasoning—in fact, we often don't realize that we are having them—and therefore are not always accurate. These inaccurate and unhelpful automatic thoughts fall under the broad categories of "cognitive distortions." You can learn more about the common types in Appendix B.

ABC MODEL OF EMOTIONS

To better understand the chain reaction of events, thoughts, and feelings, CBT uses the ABC model: an Activating situation triggers a Belief or thought, which leads to a Consequence or feeling. The activating situation or event does not inherently carry emotional content; however, the way we interpret that event through our thoughts is what causes our feelings (and also our physiological reactions and behaviors).

For instance, if you get stuck in traffic, you might react by thinking, "I'm going to be late for work and my boss will think I'm irresponsible" or "This is bad luck but there is nothing I can do about it." The former thought leads to feelings of worry or taking too much personal responsibility, whereas the latter thought leads to feelings of acceptance. Through careful identification of those automatic thoughts, you can challenge and change how your mind interprets a situation, thereby changing your emotional response.

FEEDBACK LOOPS

Your thoughts and feelings create powerful feedback loops: you likely have thoughts about your emotional reactions, which lead to more reactions (e.g. because I thought, *I can't be late!* I started to panic and this spurred more negative automatic thoughts). In this way, a negative feeling can lead to more negative thoughts, which lead to more negative feelings, and so on until we are filled with anxiety. Our bodies also develop physiological responses to these feedback loops such as increased heart rate, tightened muscles, and shorter breaths.

The combination of automatic thoughts and feedback loops can cause us to quickly develop intense and painful feelings. The core practice of CBT is being able to catch yourself as you are in an ABC chain and identifying, challenging, and replacing unhelpful automatic thoughts.

CHANGING OUR THOUGHTS

CBT is typically done with a licensed clinician, and most studies test its efficacy over 8 to 12 weeks. This notebook is not a replacement for sustained work with a therapist. However, there are CBT skills that can be learned on your own.

Below is an explanation of how your journal entries were designed to help you develop and practice these CBT skills, specifically the skill of changing your thoughts. Each journal entry asks you to describe the activating situation using just the facts, recognize your thoughts, challenge them by identifying unhelpful automatic thought patterns, and then consider alternative ways of thinking about the situation.

What happened?

Identifying the activating situation helps you understand the entire ABC chain and learn to anticipate your situational triggers and patterns. When writing the description of the activation situation, be brief and focus on specific facts. Think about whether or not an outside observer would agree with your explanation about what happened. The smaller the moment in time that you're reacting to, the more effectively you'll be able to understand the emotions and reactions that followed.

What are you thinking?

The first key step in CBT is carefully listening to and understanding your thoughts. Since automatic thoughts are registered so quickly by our minds, they can be especially difficult to observe. Try to listen to your internal dialogue by slowing it down in your mind and then recalling the thoughts you had. You may find that certain thoughts are particularly loud and stick out, or that it's very difficult to identify any thoughts. When that happens, continue probing a bit by considering if you had thoughts about yourself, or about another person, or about the environment around you.

How are you feeling?

After considering your thoughts, identify your emotions and their intensity. Pause to reflect on the relationship between these emotions and the thoughts you listed above. If you are having difficulty naming your feelings, consider the physical sensations that arose and work backwards. For example, noticing your heart rate increase and jaw clench could indicate anger or fear. Use the Feelings Wheel in Appendix C to help you accurately label your emotions.

What thinking patterns do you recognize?

Next, examine the thoughts you listed and identify the unhelpful automatic thought patterns (i.e. cognitive distortions). This process helps you reflect on how you are talking to yourself and gives you the opportunity to challenge the validity of automatic thought patterns. This skill of questioning the validity of your thoughts will help you become aware of and unlearn inaccurate ones. It is likely that many cognitive distortions will be present in a single thought. If calling out the distortions feels overwhelming, take a step back from owning the thoughts ("my thoughts") and try to find the cognitive distortions as though it were a puzzle presented to you of someone else's thoughts.

How can you think about the situation differently?

Challenging your thoughts then gives you the opportunity to compose alternative thoughts based on the available facts. These alternative thoughts will change the way you perceive situations and will therefore help you start feeling better too. Here are some helpful questions you can ask yourself to form alternative thoughts:

•   What evidence do you have? What is the most realistic conclusion to draw based on that evidence?

- When looking at this situation, what is the best possible outcome? What's the worst possible outcome? After reviewing both, what is the most realistic outcome?

- What might be a new way to look at the situation so that the impact of your perspective is positive or neutral?

- What might someone who has your best interest in mind say about this situation?

- Imagine you have the ability to "zoom out" of this situation and see it from an outside perspective. How does the situation look now?

- Imagine you are sitting with a therapist and trying to think about this situation differently. Now imagine switching roles—you are now the therapist. What would you tell your client?

WHAT TO EXPECT

Initially, these journal entries may work better as a reflection; consider completing them a few hours later or the next day after an anxiety-triggering event. When you are feeling overwhelmed, it might be too much to try to sort through thoughts and feelings in the moment. Over time, you may find that you prefer to give yourself time to regroup before reflecting on the situation, or that you prefer to do a journal entry while it's still fresh on your mind.

The benefits of CBT are realized through regular practice. While you may never be without negative automatic thoughts (we are human after all), over time you will notice that more helpful, realistic, and positive thoughts come to mind in response to an event. This will help you feel better and give you a better sense of control over your thoughts and feelings.

B   Cognitive Distortions

Cognitive distortions are a set of automatic thought patterns that are inaccurate and reinforce negative thinking or emotions. These automatic negative thoughts "distort" our thinking by leading us to believe something that is both unhelpful and untrue.

Psychiatrist and researcher Aaron Beck is credited with first proposing the theory behind cognitive distortions in the 1970s; his student, David Burns, is credited with popularizing the common names of these distortions in the 1980s. In one of his books, Burns writes: "I suspect you will find that a great many of your negative feelings are in fact based on such thinking errors"[13] given that our minds are predisposed to drawing connections between our thoughts and what we observe, it is likely that at least some of those connections are faulty and produce negative thinking.

Cognitive distortions result in negative thinking and emotions, and therefore have a negative impact on our anxiety and wellbeing. By learning to identify and challenge these logical fallacies, as you are asked to do in the journal entries, you can develop more accurate and helpful thinking patterns over time.

In this journal, we've focused on 12 of the most common cognitive distortions, listed on the next page. Note that some of these cognitive distortions are similar or related—several can apply to any given situation.

1   ALL OR NOTHING THINKING

Sometimes called polarized or black-and-white thinking, this cognitive distortion leads you to perceive things at the extremes by removing the middle ground or room for mistakes. All or nothing thinking makes the assumption that there are only two possibilities in a given situation, often expressed in "either-or" terms. Based on your actions, you may think of yourself or others as being either great or awful, hard-working or lazy, delightful or intolerable.

Example:
"I ate ice cream today so I've ruined my diet completely."

Example of reframing:
"Even while dieting, I can have foods I enjoy purely for their taste."

2   BLAMING OTHERS

Unlike self-blaming, this cognitive distortion involves holding other people entirely accountable for a negative outcome. If a bad situation must be the fault of someone else, then you are other-blaming.

Example:
"Dinner got burned because Sam left the kitchen a mess and I couldn't find anything I needed."

Example of reframing:
"Sam left the kitchen a mess—I will talk to him about cleaning up after himself. But I could have also tidied up what space and things I needed before starting dinner."

3   CATASTROPHIZING

Catastrophizing is thinking about disastrous possibilities based on a relatively small observation or event; it can lead to believing that the worst case scenario is the one that will play out.

Example:
"I botched that part of the interview; they probably will go with someone more qualified than me. I'll never get a job in my field and my student debt will have been for nothing."

Example of reframing:
"I think I answered that question poorly in the interview, but I feel good about some other responses. Hopefully this works out, but I will still have options even if it doesn't."

4   EMOTIONAL REASONING

This distortion can be summed up as, "If I feel that way, it must be true." When engaged in emotional reasoning, you accept your emotional reaction as an automatic indicator of reality. In other words, emotional reasoning occurs when you believe that something is true because of your feelings about it.

Example:
"I feel angry. This waiter must be treating me unfairly."

Example of reframing:
"I've been feeling really tired and upset today because of a few things at work. I should probably take a walk or a few deep breaths."

5   FORTUNE TELLING

Similar to mind reading, fortune telling refers to making dramatic predictions about the future with little or no evidence. Just as mind-reading overestimates our ability to know what other people are thinking, fortune-telling overestimates our ability to know what will happen in the future.

Example:
"The last relationship only lasted 2 months...this one probably will too."

Example of reframing:
"I'm going to do my best to do what I feel is right for this new relationship, regardless of how long it lasts."

6   LABELING

This cognitive distortion is an extension of overgeneralization that involves assigning negative global judgment (i.e., about an entire person or thing) based on a small amount of evidence. These labels create inaccurate views of the people, places, and things around us.

Example:
"I sent the invite to the wrong person. I'm so stupid."

Example of reframing:
"Ugh, I made a mistake and sent the invite to the wrong person. I feel pretty embarrassed."

MAGNIFYING THE NEGATIVE

Also referred to as filtering or tunnel vision, magnifying the negative fixates our thoughts on only the negative parts of a situation. By dwelling on the negative, our fears, losses, and irritations become exaggerated in importance and the positive parts of the situation not given fair consideration.

Example:
"I can't believe I included a typo in my email to HR, they are definitely going to reject my request."

Example of reframing:
"I had a typo in my email to HR, but my meaning is still clear."

MIND READING

Mind reading involves making assumptions about what others are thinking and feeling based on limited evidence. Though it is possible to have an idea of what others are thinking, these intuitions are often inaccurate because there are so many factors that influence the thoughts and feelings of others that we are not aware of.

Example:
"The cashier must think I'm some weirdo for wearing this outfit to the store."

Example of reframing:
"I feel a bit self-conscious of my outfit, but others may not notice or care."

9   MINIMIZING THE POSITIVE

Whereas magnifying the negative turns up the volume on anything bad, minimizing the positive actively reduces the volume of anything good. Specifically, this means ignoring the value or importance of the positive parts of a situation.

Example:
"Anybody could have done what I did, they're just being nice to compliment me for it."

Example of reframing:
"I did something that people find valuable and praise-worthy."

10   OVERGENERALIZATION

In overgeneralization, you draw broad conclusions based on just one piece of evidence. This thought pattern is often based on the assumption that one bad experience means that whenever you're in a similar situation, the bad experience will repeat itself. You can often identify overgeneralizations by looking for words that imply absolutes such as "all," "none," "never," and "always."

Example:
"I always get nervous and screw up presentations."

Example of reframing:
"Presentations tend to make me feel nervous."

11   SELF-BLAMING

Sometimes known as personalization, this distortion involves
believing that you are entirely responsible for a negative
situation, even for factors that are outside of your control.
Self-blaming also often assumes that what other people do or say
is a reaction to you.

Example:
"I was late to hanging out with my friend and ruined what
would've otherwise been a good time."

Example of reframing:
"I wish I hadn't been late, but it happens sometimes and I'm not
fully responsible for how she felt."

12   SHOULD STATEMENTS

Should statements involve creating narrow and inflexible rules
about how you and other people should behave. Specifically, it
means believing that you or other people "should" or "must"
act a certain way and if they do not, they are judged as faulty or
wrong in some way. This distortion imposes a set of expectations
that will very likely not be met; you feel guilty when you break
them and angry when others break them.

Example:
"I shouldn't have been so upset with her. I should have been more
calm and understanding."

Example of reframing:
"It's understandable that I felt hurt and it is helpful to communicate that. Next time, I can try to approach the situation more
calmly."

C   The Feelings Wheel

In your journal entries, you are tasked with listing the emotions you are feeling and rating their intensity. Emotions are complex—finding the right words to express them can be challenging but also very useful. Describing that you are feeling "frustrated" or "jealous" is more helpful than noting that you are feeling "bad" or "anxious" because accurately describing your emotional state will lead to an improved ability to understand, communicate, and manage that emotional state.

The Feelings Wheel on the next page is a tool used by therapists to help you quickly and accurately name the emotions you are feeling. The wheel features three rings. The inner-most ring consists of six core emotions: joy, love, fear, anger, sadness, and surprise. The outer two rings include more detailed emotions associated with these core emotions.

To use the Feelings Wheel, start by scanning all three rings of the wheel for an emotion that resonates with what you are feeling. Once you've identified that emotion, you can move toward the center of the wheel or away from the center to find the adjacent words that most accurately reflect your feelings. For instance, you might start with "sadness" and work outward to "guilty" as a more accurate feeling. Alternatively, you might start with "nervous" and work my way inward to "fear" and then outward again to "insecure" because that feels more accurate than "nervous."

The goal is not to end up at any particular ring of the feelings wheel, though people do tend to gravitate toward the outer rings of the wheel as they practice using this tool. As you're getting started, simply focus on identifying and writing down the emotions that most clearly reflect your emotional state.

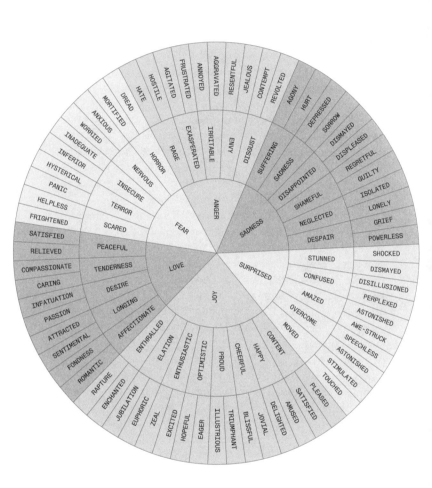

References

[1] David, D., Cristea, I. and Hofmann, S. G. (2018). Why Cognitive Behavioral Therapy Is the Current Gold Standard of Psychotherapy. *Frontiers in Psychiatry*, 9, 4. ▸ *https://doi.org/10.3389/fpsyt.2018.00004*

[2] Hofmann, S. G., Asnaani, A., Vonk, I.J., Sawyer, A.T., Fang, A. (2012). The Efficacy of Cognitive Behavioral Therapy: A Review of Meta-Analyses. *Cognitive Therapy and Research*, 36(5), 427–440. ▸ *https://doi.org/10.1007/s10608-012-9476-1*

[3] Krpan, K. M., Kross, E., Berman, M.G., Deldin, P.J., Askren M.K., Jonides, J. (2013). An Everyday Activity as a Treatment for Depression: The Benefits of Expressive Writing for People Diagnosed with Major Depressive Disorder. *Journal of Affective Disorders*, 150(3), 1148–1151. ▸ *https://doi.org/10.1016/j.jad.2013.05.065*

[4] Schleider, J. and Weisz, J. (2018). A Single-Session Growth Mindset Intervention for Adolescent Anxiety and Depression: 9-Month Outcomes of a Randomized Trial. *Journal of Child Psychology and Psychiatry*, 59(2), 160-170. ▸ *https://doi.org/10.1111/jcpp.12811*

[5] Zaccaro, A., Piarulli, A., Laurino, M., Garbella, E., Menicucci, D., Neri, B., Gemignani, A. (2018). How Breath-Control Can Change Your Life: A Systematic Review on Psycho-Physiological Correlates of Slow Breathing. *Frontiers in Human Neuroscience*, 12, 353. ▸ *https://doi.org/10.3389/fnhum.2018.00353*

[6] Ben Simon, E., Rossi, A., Harvey, A.G., Walker, M.P. (2019). Overanxious and Under-slept. *Nature Human Behavior*, 4(1), 100-110. ▸ *https://doi.org/10.1038/s41562-019-0754-8*

[7] Walker, M. P. and van der Helm, E. (2009). Overnight Therapy? The Role of Sleep in Emotional Brain Processing. *Psychological Bulletin*, 135(5), 731–748. ▸ *https://doi.org/10.1037/a0016570*

[8] Lewis, P. A., Rezaie, R., Brown, R., Roberts, N., Dunbar, R.I.M. (2011). Ventromedial Prefrontal Volume Predicts Understanding of Others and Social Network Size. *NeuroImage*, 57(4), 1624–1629. ▸ *https://doi.org/10.1016/j.neuroimage.2011.05.030*

[9] Sherman, S. M., Cheng, Y., Fingerman, K.L., Schnyer, D.M. (2015). Social Support, Stress and the Aging Brain. *Social Cognitive and Affective Neuroscience*, 11(7), 1050–1058. ▸ *https://doi.org/10.1093/scan/nsv071*

[10] Siegel, J. Z., Mathys, C., Rutledge, R.B., Crockett, M.J. (2018). Beliefs About Bad People are Volatile. *Nature Human Behaviour*, 2(10), 750–756. ▸ *https://doi.org/10.1038/s41562-018-0425-1*

[11] Inagaki, T. K., Bryne Haltom, K.E., Suzuki, S., Jevtic, I., Hornstein, E., Bower, J.E., Eisenberger, N.I. (2016). The Neurobiology of Giving Versus Receiving Support. *Psychosomatic Medicine*, 78(4), 443–453. ▸ *https://doi.org/10.1097/psy.0000000000000302*

[12] Bani Mohammad, E., and Ahmad, M. (2019). Virtual Reality as a Distraction Technique for Pain and Anxiety Among Patients with Breast Cancer: A Randomized Control Trial. Palliative and Supportive Care, 17(1), 29–34. ▸ *https://doi.org/10.1017/s1478951518000639*

[13] Burns, D. (1999). *The Feeling Good Handbook* (Rev. ed.). New York, N.Y., U.S.A.: Plume.

Journal Entries
(Continued)

1   What happened? (Describe the situation

2   What is going through your mind? (Describe the situation

3   What emotions are you feeling? (Note the intensit

1 2 3 4 5 6 7 8 9 1

1 2 3 4 5 6 7 8 9 1

1 2 3 4 5 6 7 8 9 1

4   What thought patterns do you recognize?   (Circle any or write your own)

All or nothing   Fortune telling   Minimizing the positive
Blaming others   Labeling   Overgeneralization
Catastrophizing   Magnifying the negative Self-blaming
Emotional reasoning   Mind reading   Should statements

5   How can you think about the situation differently?   (Challenge your thoughts)

NOTE FROM A THERAPIST

Practice radical self-acceptance. Avoid using these
pages to ruminate and put yourself down.

1   What happened?   (Describe the situation)

2   What is going through your mind?   (Describe the situation)

3   What emotions are you feeling?   (Note the intensity)

1 2 3 4 5 6 7 8 9 10

1 2 3 4 5 6 7 8 9 10

1 2 3 4 5 6 7 8 9 10

4   What thought patterns do you recognize?   (Circle any or write your own)

All or nothing   Fortune telling   Minimizing the positive
Blaming others   Labeling   Overgeneralization
Catastrophizing   Magnifying the negative   Self-blaming
Emotional reasoning   Mind reading   Should statements

5   How can you think about the situation differently?   (Challenge your thoughts)

NOTE FROM A THERAPIST

Our minds work at lightning speed. Take a deep
breath and try slowing down your thoughts so you
can clearly observe what you are thinking.

1   What happened?   (Describe the situation)

2   What is going through your mind?   (Describe the situation)

3   What emotions are you feeling?   (Note the intensity)

1 2 3 4 5 6 7 8 9 10

1 2 3 4 5 6 7 8 9 10

1 2 3 4 5 6 7 8 9 10

4   What thought patterns do you recognize?   (Circle any or write your own)

All or nothing   Fortune telling   Minimizing the positive
Blaming others   Labeling   Overgeneralization
Catastrophizing   Magnifying the negative   Self-blaming
Emotional reasoning   Mind reading   Should statements

5   How can you think about the situation differently?   (Challenge your thoughts)

NOTE FROM A THERAPIST

Changing a single word can challenge limiting beliefs:
instead of "I am unworthy" or "I am not enough"
practice saying "I am worthy" or "I am enough."

1   What happened?   (Describe the situation)

2   What is going through your mind?   (Describe the situation)

3   What emotions are you feeling?   (Note the intensity)

1 2 3 4 5 6 7 8 9 10

1 2 3 4 5 6 7 8 9 10

1 2 3 4 5 6 7 8 9 10

4   What thought patterns do you recognize?   (Circle any or write your own)

All or nothing   Fortune telling   Minimizing the positive
Blaming others   Labeling   Overgeneralization
Catastrophizing   Magnifying the negative   Self-blaming
Emotional reasoning   Mind reading   Should statements

5   How can you think about the situation differently?   (Challenge your thoughts)

NOTE FROM A THERAPIST

Fact-checking is a useful tool to challenge your
anxieties. What evidence is there to support
your concerns?

1   What happened?   (Describe the situation)

2   What is going through your mind?   (Describe the situation)

3   What emotions are you feeling?   (Note the intensity)

1 2 3 4 5 6 7 8 9 10

1 2 3 4 5 6 7 8 9 10

1 2 3 4 5 6 7 8 9 10

4   What thought patterns do you recognize?   (Circle any or write your own)

All or nothing   Fortune telling   Minimizing the positive
Blaming others   Labeling   Overgeneralization
Catastrophizing   Magnifying the negative Self-blaming
Emotional reasoning   Mind reading   Should statements

5   How can you think about the situation differently?   (Challenge your thoughts)

NOTE FROM A THERAPIST

If you had thought about the situation differently
in the moment, how would that have impacted how
you felt or what you chose to do?

1   What happened?   (Describe the situation)

2   What is going through your mind?   (Describe the situation)

3   What emotions are you feeling?   (Note the intensity)

1 2 3 4 5 6 7 8 9 10

1 2 3 4 5 6 7 8 9 10

1 2 3 4 5 6 7 8 9 10

4   What thought patterns do you recognize?   (Circle any or write your own)

All or nothing   Fortune telling   Minimizing the positive
Blaming others   Labeling   Overgeneralization
Catastrophizing   Magnifying the negative Self-blaming
Emotional reasoning   Mind reading   Should statements

5   How can you think about the situation differently?   (Challenge your thoughts)

NOTE FROM A THERAPIST

Imagine how differently you might behave if
you were able to catch and reframe negative
thoughts in real time.

1   What happened?   (Describe the situation)

2   What is going through your mind?   (Describe the situation)

3   What emotions are you feeling?   (Note the intensity)

1 2 3 4 5 6 7 8 9 10

1 2 3 4 5 6 7 8 9 10

1 2 3 4 5 6 7 8 9 10

4   What thought patterns do you recognize?   (Circle any or write your own)

All or nothing   Fortune telling   Minimizing the positive
Blaming others   Labeling   Overgeneralization
Catastrophizing   Magnifying the negative   Self-blaming
Emotional reasoning   Mind reading   Should statements

5   How can you think about the situation differently?   (Challenge your thoughts)

NOTE FROM A THERAPIST

In a moment of panic it can be helpful to ask
yourself: "What if everything works out?"

1   What happened?   (Describe the situation)

2   What is going through your mind?   (Describe the situation)

3   What emotions are you feeling?   (Note the intensity)

1 2 3 4 5 6 7 8 9 10

1 2 3 4 5 6 7 8 9 10

1 2 3 4 5 6 7 8 9 10

4   What thought patterns do you recognize?   (Circle any or write your own)

All or nothing   Fortune telling   Minimizing the positive
Blaming others   Labeling   Overgeneralization
Catastrophizing   Magnifying the negative   Self-blaming
Emotional reasoning   Mind reading   Should statements

5   How can you think about the situation differently?   (Challenge your thoughts)

NOTE FROM A THERAPIST

Worrying is more likely to cause problems than
solve them. Practice thinking of small steps that
will help you address your worry instead.

1   What happened?   (Describe the situation)

2   What is going through your mind?   (Describe the situation)

3   What emotions are you feeling?   (Note the intensity)

1 2 3 4 5 6 7 8 9 10

1 2 3 4 5 6 7 8 9 10

1 2 3 4 5 6 7 8 9 10

4   What thought patterns do you recognize?   (Circle any or write your own)

All or nothing   Fortune telling   Minimizing the positive
Blaming others   Labeling   Overgeneralization
Catastrophizing   Magnifying the negative   Self-blaming
Emotional reasoning   Mind reading   Should statements

5   How can you think about the situation differently?   (Challenge your thoughts)

NOTE FROM A THERAPIST

Try separating the small things from the big things.
What is going to be a good use of your time and
energy, and what can you accept or let go of?

1   What happened?   (Describe the situation)

2   What is going through your mind?   (Describe the situation)

3   What emotions are you feeling?   (Note the intensity)

1 2 3 4 5 6 7 8 9 10

1 2 3 4 5 6 7 8 9 10

1 2 3 4 5 6 7 8 9 10

4   What thought patterns do you recognize?   (Circle any or write your own)

All or nothing   Fortune telling   Minimizing the positive
Blaming others   Labeling   Overgeneralization
Catastrophizing   Magnifying the negative Self-blaming
Emotional reasoning   Mind reading   Should statements

5   How can you think about the situation differently?   (Challenge your thoughts)

NOTE FROM A THERAPIST

Approach your thoughts with more curiosity than judgment. Why did you think that? What does it do for you? What's another angle you can see it from?